# wind

### Honor Head

Copyright © QEB Publishing, Inc. 2006

First published in the United States by
QEB Publishing, Inc.
23062 La Cadena Drive
Laguna Hills, CA 92653
www.qeb-publishing.com

This edition published by
Teacher Created Resources, Inc.
6421 Industry Way
Westminster, CA 92683

www.teachercreated.com

All rights reserved. No part of this publication may be reproduced, stored in a retrieval system, or transmitted in any form or by any means, electronic, mechanical, photocopying, recording, or otherwise, without the prior permission of the publisher, nor be otherwise circulated in any form of binding or cover other than that in which it is published and without a similar condition being imposed on the subsequent purchaser.

Library of Congress Control Number: 2005911008

ISBN 978-1-4206-8103-1

Written by Honor Head
Designed by Melissa Alaverdy
Consultant Terry Jennings
Editor Hannah Ray
Picture Researcher
Joanne Forrest Smith
Illustrations Chris Davidson

Publisher Steve Evans
Editorial Director Jean Coppendale
Art Director Zeta Davies

Printed and bound in China

**Picture credits**

Key: t = top, b = bottom, c = center,
l = left, r = right, FC = front cover

**Alamy**/Roger Bamber 11, /John Henshall 10;
**Corbis**/Owen Franken 5, /Mark Gamba FC, /John Henley 8B, /Mark A Johnson 8-9, /James Marshall 6, /Roy Morsch 18-19, /Neil Rabinowitz 7, /Galen Rowell 12, /Richard Hamilton Smith 4, /Wild Country 19T, /Jim Zuckerman 13;
**Ecoscene**/Sally Morgan 15;
**Getty Images**/Martin Barraud 14, /GK & Vikki Hart 2-3, /David Tipling 17T;
**NHPA**/Stephen Dalton 16-17.

Words in **bold** can be found in the glossary on page 22.

# Contents

| | |
|---|---|
| What is wind? | 4 |
| How do we use wind? | 6 |
| Feel the breeze | 8 |
| Gale force | 10 |
| Hurricanes and tornadoes | 12 |
| Wind and plants | 14 |
| On the wing | 16 |
| Windy weather fun | 18 |
| Make a pinwheel | 20 |
| Glossary | 22 |
| Index | 23 |
| Parents' and teachers' notes | 24 |

# What is wind?

Wind is air that is moving.

You cannot see wind, but you can feel the wind on your face. You can see the wind moving clouds in the sky. You can hear the wind blowing the leaves on a tree.

The wind is blowing the plants in this field.

You can see the wind blowing the wheat in this field.

If the wind is strong, it can blow your hair around!

In hot summer weather, wind helps to keep you cool. In the winter, the wind can be very cold, and you have to wrap up when you go outside.

# How do we use wind?

We use wind for all kinds of different things.

When we hang our laundry outside, the wind helps to dry it. Wind also keeps flags flying. Without the wind, they would just hang down.

We use **wind turbines** or windmills to make electricity to light and heat people's homes. When the wind turns the blades of the turbines, they make electricity. The more the wind blows, the more electricity the turbines make.

Lots of wind turbines together are called a wind farm.

The wind helps some ships and boats to sail. The wind gets caught in the sails and pushes the ship or boat along.

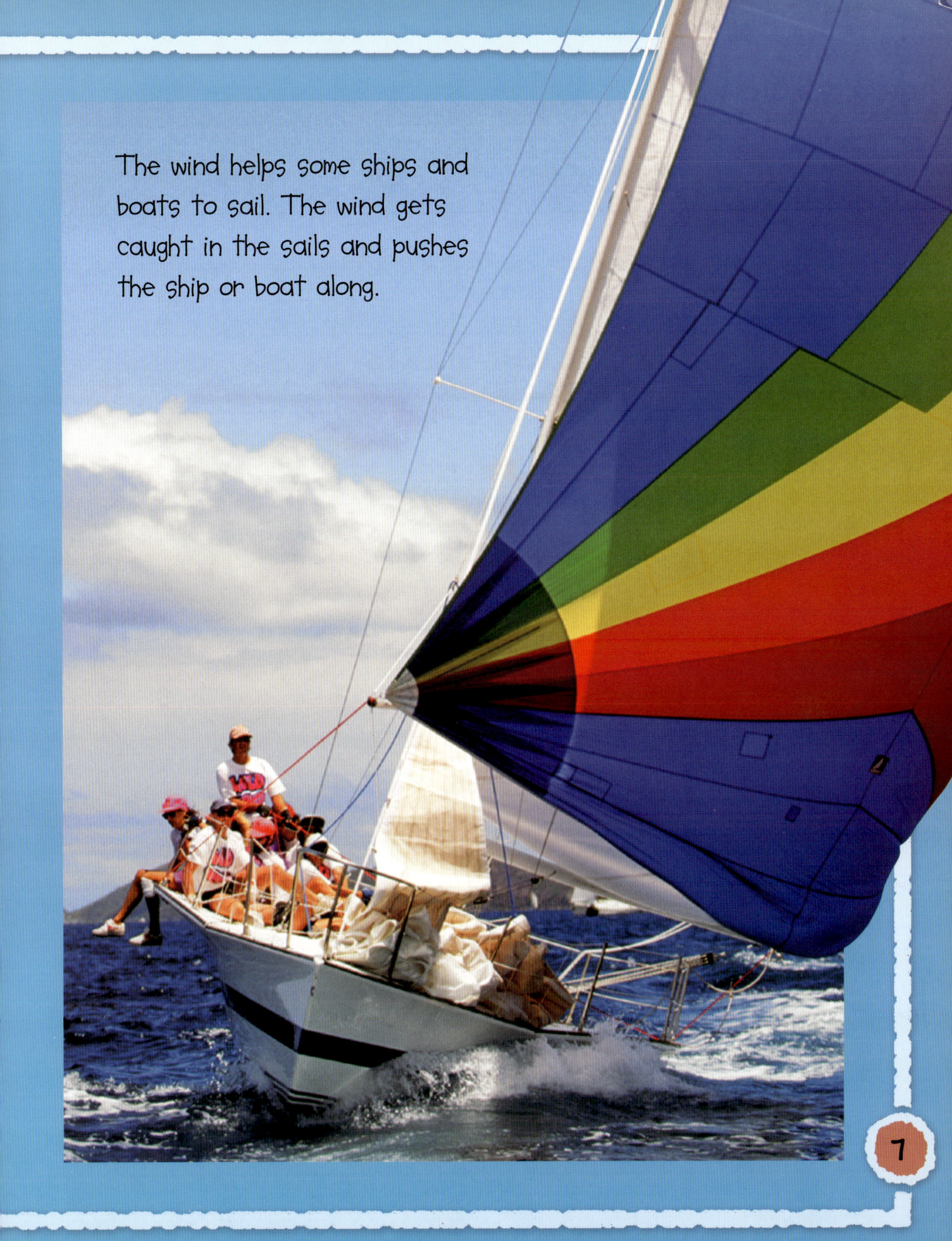

# Feel the breeze

A light wind is sometimes called a **breeze**.

A breeze may make the leaves on the trees flutter and the grass move. We usually feel a breeze on warm spring or summer days.

If you are playing outside on a warm day, a breeze helps to keep you cool.

*Sea breezes help to push windsurfers along over the water.*

When air warms up, it gets lighter and rises up into the sky. Cooler air moves in to take its place. This cooler air is the breeze that we feel.

9

# Gale force

You know there is a strong wind when the branches on the trees toss from side to side.

It can be hard to talk if a strong wind is blowing in your face. A very strong wind is called a gale.

Gales can break branches and can even blow down old trees.

A gale can make large waves on the ocean.

# Hurricanes and tornadoes

Some winds are so strong thay they can cause a lot of damage.

Large storms with powerful winds and heavy rain are called hurricanes. A hurricane forms when **storm clouds** build up over warm ocean water and get bigger and bigger.

A hurricane is strong enough to blow down houses and turn cars upside down.

Tornadoes can travel across the land at speeds of up to 75 mph (120 km/h).

WARNING!
It is dangerous to be out during a hurricane or a tornado.

A tornado is a narrow funnel of extremely strong wind that hangs down from a dark thundercloud and touches the ground. This swirling cloud is like a vacuum cleaner—it sucks up everything in its path.

# Wind and plants

Many plants need the wind to help them spread their pollen or seeds.

To make new plants, **pollen** from one flower has to move to another flower of the same kind. This is usually done by bees and other insects, but some plants use the wind to spread their pollen.

Dandelion seeds are spread when the wind blows on the plant. The seeds float in the air and land in the soil, where they grow into new plants.

Some trees and plants have special seeds that use the wind to travel and spread. These seeds are very light and are easily picked up by the wind and carried away.

Trees such as this sycamore have seeds with wings. The wings help the seeds to stay in the air longer and travel farther.

# On the wing

Animals also make use of the wind. Many large birds use the wind to help them fly.

Birds with big wings, such as this bald eagle, use the wind to help lift them into the air.

This sea albatross uses its long, narrow wings to float on the wind just above the ocean. It can travel a long way like this.

Birds can use their large wings to help them **glide** on the wind for many miles. This means they don't have to flap their wings as much, so they don't get tired.

# Windy weather fun

There are lots of fun things you can do using the wind.

Many people go to the top of a hill to fly kites, because the wind is usually stronger up high.

The wind helps to lift your kite into the air.

People who go paragliding and hang-gliding use the wind like birds. They glide through the air on the wind.

# Make a pinwheel

Make a pinwheel and see the wind move for yourself.

1. Decide how big you want your pinwheel to be and find a square of construction paper that size. You will also need a thin piece of wood for the handle of your pinwheel.

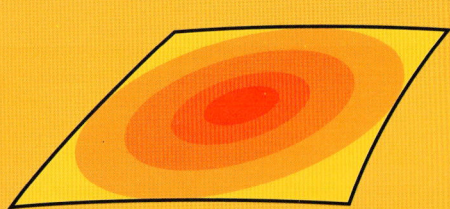

2. Paint or draw a bright pattern on both sides of your square of paper. Fold your square, corner to corner, then unfold. Fold the other two corners together, and unfold again.

3. Make a pencil mark along the fold lines, about halfway from the center of the square.

4. Cut along the fold lines, stopping at your pencil marks. Fold each point into the center of the pinwheel. Ask an adult to push a thumbtack through all four points to hold the corners together.

5. Turn the wheel to make sure it will spin around the thumbtack.

6. Push the thumbtack into the top of the handle.

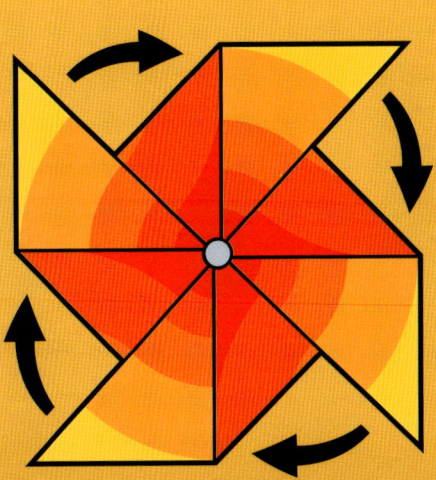

7. Stand in the wind and watch your pinwheel spin.

# Glossary

**breeze** — a light wind that you usually feel on a hot summer day

**glide** — when a bird moves through the air without flapping its wings
It uses the wind to push it along

**pollen** — the yellow dust inside flowers that helps the plant to grow new seeds

**storm clouds** — tall, dark clouds that usually bring heavy rain and strong winds

**wind turbines** — tall, white towers with blades that are turned by the wind to make electricity
They look a little like windmills

# Index

albatross 17

bald eagle 16
bees 14
birds 16–17
breeze 8–9, 22

clouds 4, 12, 13

dandelion seeds 14

electricity 6

flags 6

gales 10–11
glide 17, 19, 22

hang-gliding 19
hurricanes 12–13

insects 14

kites 18

laundry 6

ocean 11–12

paragliding 19
pinwheel 20–21
plants 14–15
pollen 14, 22

rain 12

sailboats 7
seeds 14–15
storm clouds 12, 22
sycamore 15

thunderclouds 13
tornadoes 13
trees 10, 15

waves 11–12
wind:
  having fun in 18–19
  how it helps plants 14–15
  how we use it 6–7
  seeing it move 4, 10, 20
  very light 8–9
  very strong 12–13
  what it is 4–5
wind farm 6
windmills 6
wind turbines 6, 22
windsurfing 9
wings 15–17

23

# Parents' and teachers' notes

- Look at the cover of the book. Discuss the title and the picture on the cover. What do the children expect to see in the book? Are they looking forward to reading the book?
- Look through the book. Point out the captions to the photographs. Explain that captions give us more information about the photos.
- Find the contents, glossary, and index pages. Explain the purpose of these to the children.
- Talk about the different types of wind. What is the wind like today? Look out of the window. Are the clouds moving quickly? Can you see trees moving? What else can you see that is being moved by the wind?
- Which season do the children associate with wind? For example, summer breezes or fall wind blowing the leaves off trees.
- Do the children like the wind? Is it fun? Scary? Uncomfortable?
- Talk about how the children know it is windy. When can they hear it/see it/feel it?
- Choose a selection of different-weight cloth items such as wool scarves, cotton handkerchiefs or headscarves, dish towels, and bath towels. On a windy day, take them outside and ask the children to hold up the materials. Which ones fly in the wind? Do the same experiment when the wind is stronger or weaker. If the wind is stronger, do the heavier materials start to fly?
- Point out that the wind does not always come from the same direction. Look for weather vanes and windsocks. Make a model weather vane or windsock.
- Draw a sky full of kites. Ask each child to draw and decorate a kite and put them all up on the wall against a blue-sky background. Add strings to each kite.